LIFE
IN THE
WILD

Written by Lizzie Daly

Illustrated by Chiara Fedele

CONTENTS

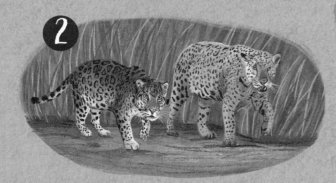

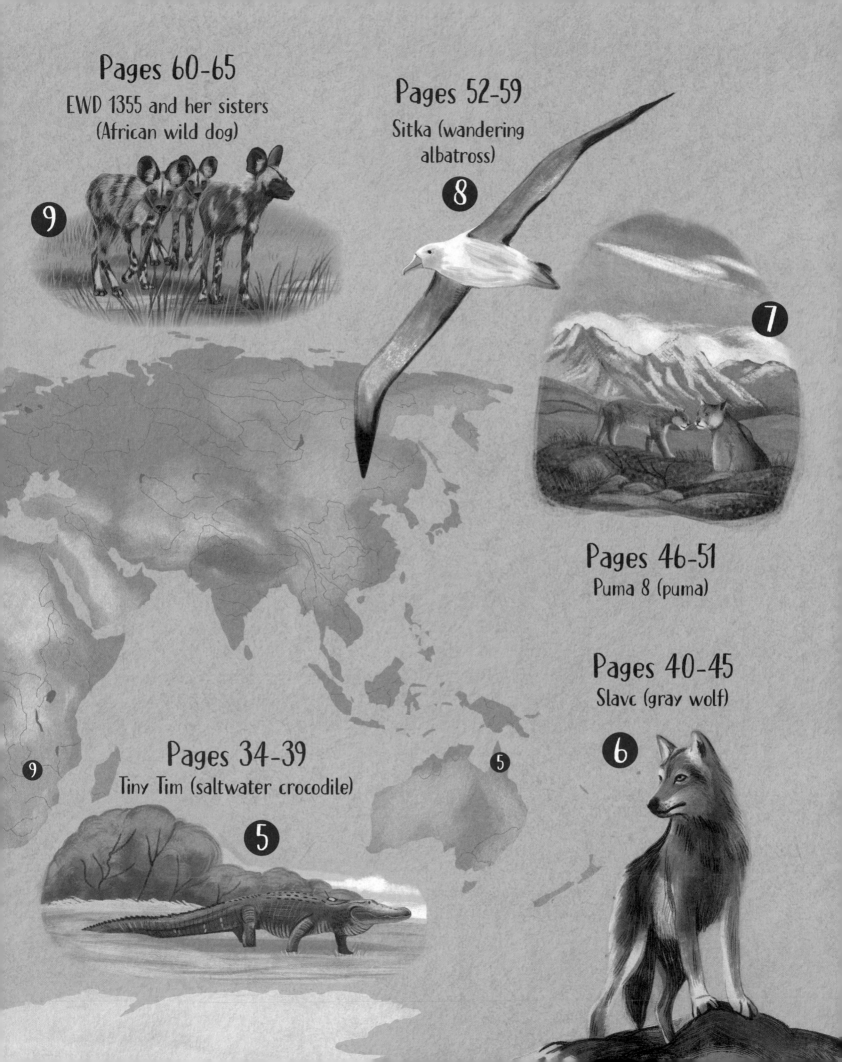

"She was a good mom, keeping a healthy cub close by her side, but in a world of melting ice a mammoth journey was about to begin."

Location: Alaska

Species: Polar bear

Ursus maritimus

Polar bear 20741

The big swim

Polar bear 20741 is a healthy, adult female weighing in at more than 485 lb (220 kg) who calls the Alaska Beaufort Sea coast her home. In August 2008, she, along with her yearling female cub, were collared for tracking. This is where their story begins. One day, they both headed for the open ocean and began to swim. Minutes turned to hours. Hours turned to days...

20741's swim

The mother and her cub kept swimming. They headed for places that should have had sea ice, but, instead, were just open water. Polar bears typically swim between land and ice floes to hunt seal prey in the Arctic. Due to rising temperatures and warming seas, however, polar bears such as 20741 are having to swim farther than ever to find food or a suitable habitat.

2

The journey began here.

Beaufort Sea

1

RUSSIA

1 leaving dry land

Having raised a healthy young cub, 20741 still needed to hunt for food from her chilly home on the Alaskan coast. This mother's instinct set the long and exhausting journey into motion.

2 Out on the water

Luckily, conditions were quite calm during her swim, with a flat sea and low winds. 20741 also swam with the sea currents and in relatively warm waters—between 35-43°F (2-6°C). This is probably how she survived the enormous journey.

Arctic Ocean

❸ Finding land

Nine days later, 20741 finally hauled her now-exhausted body onto pack ice. She had swum for a total of 232 continuous hours, logging 427 miles (687 km). When she eventually found land, 20741 had lost 22 percent of her total body fat.

After nine days, 20741 found land.

❸

❹

Alaska,

USA

CANADA

❹ The cost of the swim

When 20741 then began her 1,120 mile (1,800 km) journey on foot, only one set of footprints was left behind. Although polar bears are really well adapted to swim for long journeys, a distance of this magnitude is rare. As 20741 headed off into the distance, the loss of her cub reminds us how these iconic bears are facing growing challenges every day.

Gulf of Alaska

Polar bears

Polar bears are dependent on the sea ice for hunting, resting, mating, and denning. When they are not on the ice, polar bears are strong swimmers. There are reports of polar bears swimming at least 40 miles (64 km) in one trip.

The small ears are an adaptation to help conserve body heat.

Life on the ice

Polar bears live in icy Arctic regions such as Canada and Russia. They spend most of their time on the sea ice, raising cubs and hunting for food. But they are also so well-adapted to life in the ocean that they are classed as marine mammals.

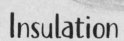

Insulation

Polar bears are so well insulated that they have to be careful not to overheat. They have black skin and their hairs are transparent, but appear white. Their fur is water repellent, and the structure of the individual hairs **channels solar energy directly into their skin beneath.** Under the fur, the black skin absorbs this energy better than lighter skin would, helping the polar bear to stay warm.

Diet

The diet of polar bears consists mainly of ringed and bearded seals. The bears patiently wait by the seals' breathing holes carved in the ice, using their powerful sense of smell to detect their prey heading up for air. **Polar bears need to eat approximately 50-75 seals a year to survive**, relying on the high fat content of the seal blubber to contribute to their own thick layer of warm fat.

A polar bear's fur turns yellow with age.

Master predator

Polar bears are the **world's largest land carnivores**. Males reach lengths of 8 ft (2.5 m), while females are smaller. Their weight varies throughout the year, but adult males can weigh up to 1,750 lb (800 kg). On land, they can reach speeds of 25 mph (40 kph) when sprinting short distances to catch large prey, such as caribou and musk oxen.

The forepaws are paddle-like and partially webbed for swimming.

Polar bear conservation

Before the 21st century, some ice caps remained frozen during the summer over the continental shelf in the Beaufort Sea. However, recent summer melts have made conditions in the Arctic increasingly more unpredictable for polar bears, with ice-free summers predicted by 2100. Their dependency on sea ice makes these bears one of the species most at risk from climate change.

The melting sea ice

20741's journey suggests that long-distance swimming efforts like this are a behavioral response to declining sea-ice conditions. This is tricky, mainly because this type of movement uses more energy than traveling over sea ice on foot. **Not only do the longer hunting journeys take their toll on the bears' own energy, but they also make it more likely that young cubs will be lost to exhaustion.** Scientists expect that as their numbers continue to decline, the population of polar bears could decrease by more than 30 percent by 2050 without any intervention.

Journal entry

The sounds of icy winds and cracking ice fill the bay. It's 5°F (-15°C), and as I glance down at my watch in the bright sunlight, it reads 2am. Here in the archipelago of Svalbard in the Arctic, there is 24-hour daylight in the summer months. I find myself leaning hard over the side of the expedition vessel, gripping onto the cold metal with my bare hands. My heart is racing.

In front of me on the coastline is a huge male polar bear. He's traveling along the edge, sniffing the air as he goes. He throws each limb forward, parting the sand like a wave, one massive paw at a time. With each lift of his leg, I get a glimpse of his black paw pads. I can almost hear his breath as he pulls his heavy body forward.

The polar bear stops at the water's edge, puts his head down, and with no effort at all, plunges into the inky water. Snow flurries up behind him. That dense white fur now looks like a heavy white curtain draped over his dark skin. The male turns toward us, using his nose as a compass for direction. Under the water, his powerful paws propel him with ease. This is where polar bears thrive. They can travel at great speeds when swimming. Until you have seen a polar bear with your very own eyes, it's impossible to describe the presence they hold. They're not just bears, but kings and queens of the Arctic wilderness.

Protecting the population

The overall decline of body condition, survival, and population sizes of polar bears has been directly linked to changes in sea-ice conditions. **By collaring these bears, scientists aim to better understand how numbers are being impacted** and try and forecast population trends so that the bears can be protected for the future. **Tracking den sites is crucial in monitoring population numbers.** Mapping these sites is also important, since the bears have to travel farther afield in the search for food and, so, in some locations, encounter more humans than ever before.

Location: The Pantanal

Species: Jaguar

Panthera onca

Mango

The clash for power

In the world's largest tropical wetland area, there lives a unique jaguar named Mango. He is a mighty male weighing more than 220 lb (100 kg). Mango was one of the first male jaguars to be collared by a team of scientists in the wilds of the Pantanal, in South America. The team hoped to find out what it was like for a male fighting for dominance. Defending his territory was very important, especially in Mango's home, where there were so many other jaguars nearby.

"Mango's striking yellow eyes and distinctive rosette patterns on his head allowed the local team to identify him."

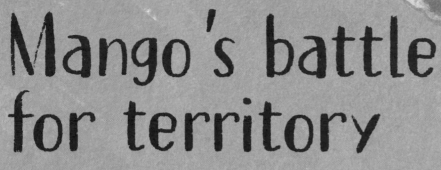

Mango's battle for territory

Some time ago, Tupah, a huge dominant male, roamed the Pantanal. Then one day, he disappeared, never to be seen again. With Tupah gone, the title for dominance was up for grabs. Would Mango take his place? Males reach maturity at around three years old, and with Mango approaching that age, he was a great contender. But the Pantanal is a vast area, and he was not alone...

The fight

Each night, Mango went on the hunt for food. On one particular evening, as he slunk through the long grass at the edge of his territory, he came across **another male, Suki.** Suki matched Mango in both size and strength, and an almighty fight took place. It was so intense that the thick collar on Mango's neck was completely ripped off.

The Pantanal

This ecosystem is bursting with wildlife, and different species come and go with the patterns of the wet and dry seasons. **The Pantanal landscape is made up of open grasslands, wetlands, and patches of dense "hammock forests."** Some jaguars like to spend their time in the open areas, while others use the forest to their advantage.

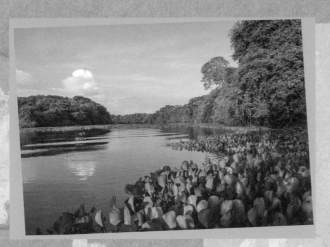

BRAZIL

The Pantanal

The aftermath

The fight was over in seconds, but it was so powerful that the males rose many feet off the ground as they threw themselves at one another. Despite its durability, this collar, ripped from Mango by Suki, shows just how strong these jaguars can be.

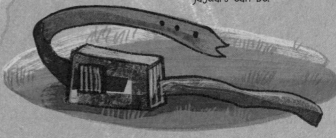

What have we learned?

GPS collars allow scientists to understand new things about this elusive species. Mango's fight for dominance was intense, but he persevered, and he is still a strong and successful predator. After the fight with Suki, Mango, now with cuts and scars on his face, limped away into the wilderness. **Scientists followed his movements closely and tracked him to a new area with thick bush and hammock forests.** It is still unknown whether he will return to his former territory and become the next dominant male or whether he will move on in search of a new kingdom.

Jaguars

Jaguars are the largest cats in the Americas. They are nimble and powerful and slink effortlessly across rough terrain and through water and thick forest. Their black and orange spots, known as "rosettes", make them masters of disguise. Each jaguar has its own unique rosettes that can be used to identify them.

Built for their habitat

Jaguars in the Pantanal are bigger than jaguars in the Amazon Rainforest. In the Amazon, they have to be lighter and more nimble so they can move easily through the dense habitat.

Keystone species

Jaguars are what is known as a keystone species, which means they play an important role in **controlling the populations** of other species, helping to keep the ecosystem in balance.

The rosettes are distinctive.

The broad feet have retractable claws.

Jaguars have the strongest bite force of any big cat in the world, and can pierce through the skull or shell of their prey.

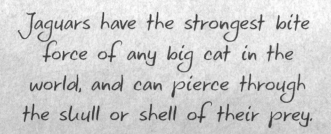

Staking their claim

Jaguars are, for the most part, solitary creatures. Although their territories often overlap with other jaguars, they know to keep away, thanks to a series of roars, scrapes, and urine markings. While not common, males do sometimes clash over territory and females.

Skillful swimmers

Unlike most other cats, jaguars do not avoid water, and, in fact, are very good swimmers. Rivers provide prey in the form of fish, turtles, and caimans. Their large paws are perfect for navigating muddy ground and act as swimming paddles. Jaguars hunt both by day and at night and travel up to 6 miles (10 km) when hunting. **They are also strong climbers** that can scale trees to stalk their prey.

Giant paws, like paddles, are good for swimming.

Jaguar conservation

Outside this protected area of the Pantanal, jaguars face conflict with humans, habitat loss through deforestation, and the risk of poachers. In recent years, there has also been a change in the typical wet and dry seasons, making the climate of their habitats unstable.

Safe haven

There is still a lot we don't know about wild jaguars. But from collaring work, such as with Mango, scientists are able to build up a picture of the lives of jaguars in the wild. Conservation teams have worked hard to protect this area, and as a result, this reserve has one of the highest densities of jaguars seen anywhere on the planet. **While there are still fights over territory and resources, for now, the Pantanal remains a safe haven for this elusive but charismatic species.**

Journal entry

As the sun starts to set and the land becomes golden, the flooded fields glisten in the light and the hyacinth macaws squawk as they head home to roost for the night. The pulsing sound of the Pantanal at nighttime starts to fill the air. Dwarf frogs call as Mango slinks through the long grass. As Mango traces the edge of his territory, I watch through my binoculars in awe.

Mango has a real presence. His shoulders, flank, and back are peppered with beautiful rosette patterns of all different shapes and sizes. His fur is a golden yellow, which matches his striking yellow eyes. His distinctive eyes and the rosette patterns on his head help the local team ID him.

He rests with his mouth slightly open as he pants in the sun. His true strength is visible from the size of his head. He is just a few years old, but this young male means business. As part of the research, Mango was collared so that scientists could observe his whereabouts and find out whether he will be the first male to move for dominance in the area.

As Mango moves through the landscape from flooded open grassland to the hammock forest, he is flehmening (curling out the upper lip to detect scents in the air), urinating, and scraping trees. He is marking his territory while searching for prey—armadillos, deer, or even yacare caimans. As the sun dips below the horizon, the Pantanal is quiet once more.

Jaguars across the world

In Brazil, jaguars are considered a vulnerable species. Their global population is estimated to be around 173,000, with about 86,000 in Brazil alone. **The jaguar has already lost 50 percent of its historical range across the Americas.** Currently, the species occupies approximately half of its original distribution (which extended from southeastern North America to south-central Argentina). **Overall, the Amazon Basin and the Pantanal region are considered strongholds,** harboring the largest estimated populations of jaguars, which, therefore, have the highest probability of long-term survival.

- **Location:** Bermuda
- **Species:** Tiger shark
- *Galeocerdo cuvier*

Harry Lindo
The well-traveled tiger shark

Meet Harry Lindo. He traveled one of the longest tracked distances ever recorded for a tiger shark when he embarked on a journey of more than 27,000 miles (43,000 km) around the ocean. Despite tiger sharks being well-known apex predators in our oceans (with no natural predators of their own), much of their movements and behaviors were a mystery. They were long thought to be mainly a coastal species, but because of Harry Lindo, we now know they are long-distance travelers.

"On Harry Lindo's long-distance trip, he spent months on end in various locations across the deep."

Harry Lindo's migration

Tiger sharks are one of our ocean's most iconic and recognizable predators, but before this study many of their habits were mysterious to scientists, and their movements were hard to track. However, when some sharks, including Harry Lindo, were tagged and tracked for more than three years, they offered scientists a detailed look at their long-distance migratory patterns for the very first time...

USA

Tiger sharks are opportunistic, and they are mighty. Some are migratory, and others are residents.

What have we learned?

To help scientists protect tiger sharks, it is extremely important that we **understand their movements**. The researchers of this study managed to build a picture of shark movements in the Atlantic Ocean, which is a great step toward effective conservation. Harry Lindo's hugely long journey revealed remarkable and **previously unknown migratory patterns**, more in line with turtles, some marine mammals, and even birds than with many species of shark.

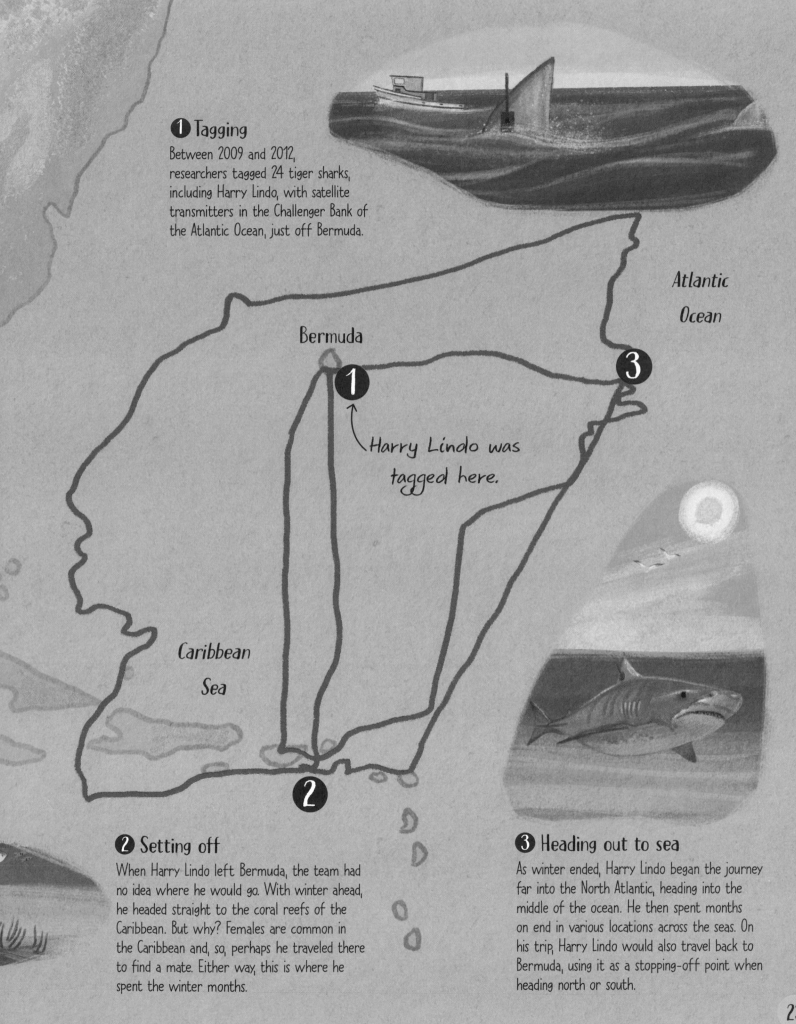

❶ Tagging

Between 2009 and 2012, researchers tagged 24 tiger sharks, including Harry Lindo, with satellite transmitters in the Challenger Bank of the Atlantic Ocean, just off Bermuda.

Bermuda

Atlantic Ocean

Harry Lindo was tagged here.

Caribbean Sea

❷ Setting off

When Harry Lindo left Bermuda, the team had no idea where he would go. With winter ahead, he headed straight to the coral reefs of the Caribbean. But why? Females are common in the Caribbean and, so, perhaps he traveled there to find a mate. Either way, this is where he spent the winter months.

❸ Heading out to sea

As winter ended, Harry Lindo began the journey far into the North Atlantic, heading into the middle of the ocean. He then spent months on end in various locations across the seas. On his trip, Harry Lindo would also travel back to Bermuda, using it as a stopping-off point when heading north or south.

Tiger sharks

Tiger sharks belong to one of the largest families of sharks, called requiem sharks. These sharks are mostly found in warm ocean waters, where they actively hunt a large variety of prey using their bladelike teeth.

The large mouth has big, sharp teeth.

A solitary life

Tiger sharks are solitary animals, but they will **feed with other sharks if large prey is available.** Spending their time in deeper waters during the day, they move closer to shore at night to hunt. Tiger sharks also come together in groups during mating season. In the Northern Hemisphere, mating takes place in spring. In the Southern Hemisphere, it happens during winter.

Spots to stripes

Females mate once every three years. After 12-16 months, they give birth to litters of around 30 pups. The pups are born 18-35 in (46-89 cm) long and are fully independent. Instead of stripes, **pups have gray spots.** As they grow older, these develop into the stripes that give tiger sharks their name. After a certain age, the stripes begin to fade.

The stripes develop with age.

The long upper tail can provide a burst of speed when necessary.

A powerful, torpedo-shaped body cuts through the water.

Eating habits

These sharks are quick and agile hunters with big appetites. Tiger sharks in particular have gained a reputation for their feeding habits; they eat almost anything, earning them the nickname **"the garbage can of the sea."** They feed on sea snakes, clams, crabs, squid, fish, sharks, rays, turtles, seals, dolphins, birds, and even human trash.

Powerful night vision

Just like the tigers they are named after, tiger sharks have excellent night vision. Their eyesight in dim light is roughly 10 times better than a human's. This is helped by a layer of reflective tissue behind the retina of their eye, called the tapetum.

Shark conservation

While no one fully understands why Harry Lindo makes his trip around the world every year, what we do know from his journey is that this shark species is adaptable enough to live in two vastly different ecosystems across seasons.

About the study

The study was led by James Lea and Brad Wetherbee, PhD, co-first authors, and senior author, Mahmood Shivji, PhD, all of whom work out of Nova Southeastern University's (NSU) Guy Harvey Research Institute in Florida. Renowned marine artist and conservationist Guy Harvey, a PhD fisheries ecologist, co-led the project's tagging work. This took place near Bermuda in collaboration with the Bermuda Shark Project. **By tagging and understanding movements from year to year, scientists can identify breeding and feeding hotspots** as well as shark highways.

Journal entry

The sun glistens off the ocean. A large dorsal fin slices through the surface of the water and then sinks down into the blue. As I take my last breath, I push myself forward and start to sink down through the water column, with the drumming sound of the boat engine fading away. I power down with my long diving fins, heading straight for the seafloor and, at 16 ft (5 m) deep, I turn. There, swimming alongside me, is the silhouette of an adult tiger shark.

Her enormous body is two times the length of mine. Stripes of silver along her flank glisten in the light. She glides through the water effortlessly in a swim behavior known as "roller-coaster swimming." Like a rollercoaster, she moves up and down the water column, and this is one of the more efficient ways of swimming. As she rises above me, her white underbelly glows through the gloomy deep blue, her size and form looking even more impressive.

My lungs are starting to burn, but I want to get closer, so, with just a few more kicks, I push even harder in her direction. As she sinks back down the water column, there I am, eye to eye with her. Her enormous, inky-dark eye flicks back and forth, looking right back at me. No bubbles, no other humans-just the two of us swimming side by side, surrounded only by the sound of the ocean. A magical moment with a true predator of the sea.

Spanning the oceans

When you have a species that covers such huge distances, facing so many different threats along the way, being able to protect it from the scale of the problems can be a real challenge. **Understanding how these tiger sharks use the oceans, however, is the first step toward effective conservation.** In addition, we can learn more about how these marine environments are changing. More recently, it's thought that due to warming waters, tiger sharks are moving farther north into areas previously uninhabited by this species. **This could put the whole marine ecosystem out of balance** because they are now feeding on new species.

Location: Antarctica

Species: Leopard seal

Hydrurga leptonyx

Bigonia

The leopard seal that's pushing boundaries

Meet Bigonia, the largest female leopard seal ever tracked by scientists. In 2022, she made not only one of the longest recorded journeys of its kind, but also demonstrated some of the deepest dives along the way. While this is her story, she was just one of many female leopard seals tracked in Antarctica.

" Bigonia is part of a study by scientists, who are in a race against time to understand how adaptable this species is in a rapidly changing climate. "

SOUTH
AMERICA

Bigonia's loop

Deep down in the Southern Ocean lives a predator with a real reputation. Bigonia lives a solitary life, hunting and traveling alone. However, she also needs somewhere suitable to give birth. So, in 2022, she embarked on a mammoth journey.

Atlantic Ocean

Bigonia was tagged here, at Cape Shirreff.

1

1 Tagging

Bigonia was tagged along with 21 other seals by scientists looking at how leopard seals survive in extreme polar conditions. Like a lot of leopard seals found in Cape Shirreff, on the West Antarctic peninsula, she is a summer resident. Cape Shirreff's shores come alive with penguin chicks and Antarctic fur seal pups in the summer months, making this the perfect hunting ground.

ANTARCTICA

Southern Ocean

Large and in charge

Bigonia weighs in at a massive 1,190 lb (540 kg) and is over 10 ft (3 m) long. Another female in the study weighed just 730 lb (330 kg). Bigonia has several scars on her body, which are likely from aggressive encounters with other leopard seals over the years. She was given the "big" in her name because of her enormous size, traveling further and diving deeper than any of the other seals in the study.

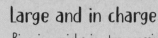

Scotia Sea

South Georgia

❷ Champion swimmer and diver

Some leopard seals traveled less than 30 miles (50 km) from the base, whereas Bigonia crossed the Southern Ocean, logging a whopping 1,037 miles (1,669 km), all the way to the far flung island of South Georgia. Crossing wild open seas and diving down to extreme depths of more than 2,300 ft (700 m) for food, she ventured solo. Scientists think she did this to find a suitable habitat for giving birth, showing how important it is to protect these environments.

What have we learned?

Bigonia has shown us that **there is a lot we do not know about leopard seals.** They had otherwise been considered pretty unimpressive divers, with short and shallow depths being most common during their time at sea. Bigonia, however, showed us that **they do push their dives,** sometimes down to **2,300 ft (700 m).** This knowledge can help us learn where leopard seals are hunting for different types of prey and how that changes over time. Bigonia also proved that there are large variations in the lengths of their journeys out at sea.

Leopard seals

As one of Antarctica's dominant predators, the leopard seal plays an important role in the region's ecosystem and food chain. They are intelligent, powerful, and solitary animals that survive due to their curiosity and adaptability.

Unlike other seals

Leopard seals have powerful front flippers that help to propel them through the water, making them unusually agile compared to other seals. Despite the harsh and extreme conditions in which they live, leopard seals have a long life expectancy than many other seals. This is mainly due to the fact they have just one predator—the orca. If they manage to avoid predation, they can reach up to 25 years old.

The leopard seal has earned its name due to the spotted, mottled appearance of its fur coat.

Each leopard seal has its own unique pattern, which helps scientists identify and learn more about individuals.

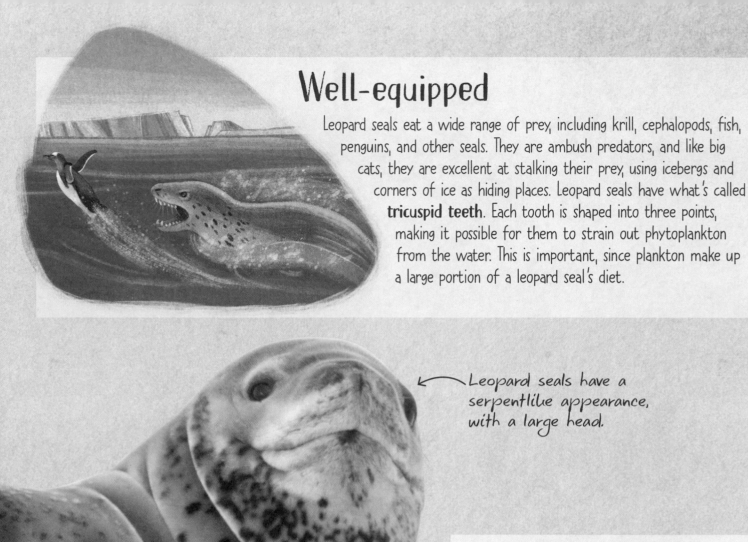

Well-equipped

Leopard seals eat a wide range of prey, including krill, cephalopods, fish, penguins, and other seals. They are ambush predators, and like big cats, they are excellent at stalking their prey, using icebergs and corners of ice as hiding places. Leopard seals have what's called **tricuspid teeth**. Each tooth is shaped into three points, making it possible for them to strain out phytoplankton from the water. This is important, since plankton make up a large portion of a leopard seal's diet.

Leopard seals have a serpentlike appearance, with a large head.

Sexual dimorphism

Female leopard seals are 50 percent larger than males. This size difference between males and females in the animal kingdom is called **sexual dimorphism**. Females spend a significantly longer amount of time on land and ice than males do. Scientists believe this is largely to give birth and to look after young pups.

"Tiny Tim is an estuarine crocodile, which means he inhabits the salty waters of wetlands and marine areas, where land meets sea."

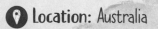 **Location:** Australia

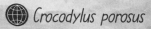 **Species:** Saltwater crocodile

🌐 *Crocodylus porosus*

Tiny Tim

The long journey home

In August 2014, scientists got a call about a crocodile called Tiny Tim. But at more than 770 lb (350 kg), he was far from tiny. He lived in Cape York in Queensland, Australia, on the Steve Irwin Wildlife Reserve. He was causing issues as he was getting too close to a local town. Crocodiles can be dangerous to humans, so it was important the team moved him away from people. This is the story of how this clever reptile was flown in a helicopter over 250 miles (400 km) away, only for him to be able to navigate his own way back home!

Tiny Tim's journey

At his new home, Tiny Tim would have a wild, open space to inhabit, away from built-up communities. However, he had other ideas. After just a few months, he started the journey back. By riding currents, he took fewer than 20 days to return the 250 miles (400 km) home, using tidal movements of waterways to journey all the way back.

Queensland,

AUSTRALIA

1

Tiny Tim was tagged here.

2

3

Steve Irwin Wildlife Reserve

❶ Relocation and tagging

After relocating Tiny Tim via helicopter to a less-populated area, scientists then attached a specially designed location transmitter to the back of his head. This allowed them to track his movements, and it certainly paid off when they were able to witness how he cleverly swam back home.

2 Traveling solo

250 miles (400 km) away from his home, Tiny Tim was out in the wilderness. Little did scientists know that he decided to embark upon the journey back! Using tides and currents, he was on the move.

Saltwater crocodiles can also be found in freshwater environments.

3 Home again

Tiny Tim's long journey included impressive daily movements of 6-18 miles (10-30 km). He would even use the position of the sun and magnetic fields to navigate. After just 20 days, he found himself back home. Studying Tim, it is clear that estuarine crocodiles can exhibit strong site fidelity, which means the ability to return to a previously known location.

What have we learned?

Tiny Tm's story is a great example of how **these prehistoric animals are masters of navigation.** They have strong site fidelity and use the environment and their senses to travel huge distances. **However, it's also a story of growing conflict between humans and crocodiles in shared habitats.** It indicates that relocating crocodiles to a new area is not the best management tool for reducing conflict with people. As more and more people push up against the habitat of crocodiles, we need to find a way to co-exist with this species.

Saltwater crocodiles

Saltwater crocodiles are known to be fantastic swimmers and are able to travel long distances—there have even been multiple reports of these animals spotted in the open ocean, far from land.

Crocodiles have the largest bite force of any animal.

Constant alert

Saltwater crocodiles are capable of unihemispheric sleep. This means they shut down just one half of their brain at a time, keeping the other half awake and alert to danger. Their central nervous system is wired to keep one eye open at all times so they can avoid any surprise attacks.

Skillful hunters

Saltwater crocodiles are nocturnal hunters, and they will pounce on any animal they can capture—including humans, and even other saltwater crocodiles. They often surprise unsuspecting prey by emerging from below the surface and pulling it into the water to eat it. They are known for using the **"death roll"** with larger prey, where they spin their prey in the water rapidly, disorienting it, and breaking it apart into smaller, digestible pieces.

Crocodiles have been on Earth for millions of years.

A valve at the bottom of the mouth seals off the throat, so the croc can open its mouth underwater without drowning.

Massive reptiles

Saltwater crocodiles are the **largest** and **heaviest** of the world's reptiles. They have been known to weigh up to 2,650 lb (1,200 kg). Males range from 7½-11 ft (2.3-3.3 m) in length and weigh somewhere in the range of 330-660 lb (150-300 kg). **Males are about a third larger than females** in terms of size and weight—saltwater crocodiles have one of the biggest size differences between the sexes when it comes to animal species.

"Slavc was one of an estimated 4,000 wolves living on the Balkan peninsula of Europe. His perilous journey took him through every kind of habitat, from forests, to suburban streets, and mountain peaks."

Location: Europe

Species: Gray wolf

Canis lupus

Slavc

The wolf in search of love

Slavc is a gray wolf who was fitted with a radio collar so that scientists could track his movements. To their surprise, Slavc embarked on an almost 1,250 mile (2,000 km) journey across Europe. Eventually, Slavc found a mate and had pups, bringing together two wolf populations that had been separated for more than 150 years.

Slavc's journey

In the depths of winter, in December 2011, Slavc began a long journey after leaving his home range in the southwest of Slovenia. He was in search of one thing—a female wolf. However, little did Slavc know, he would face huge challenges along the way...

Alps

4 Entering Italy

Slavc then hit the Italian Alps, where more than 1,000 wolves can be found. The GPS movements showed scientists that he had spent 12 days there before continuing his journey farther into Italy.

ITALY

5 Meeting Giulietta

The team tracking Slavc noticed there were two sets of tracks in the snow. After nearly two years, it appeared that Slavc had found a female wolf, named Giulietta, to mate with.

6 Starting a pack

In their first reproductive season in 2013, Slavc and Giulietta produced five cubs. Then in 2014, they added another seven to the pack, with seven more following in 2015.

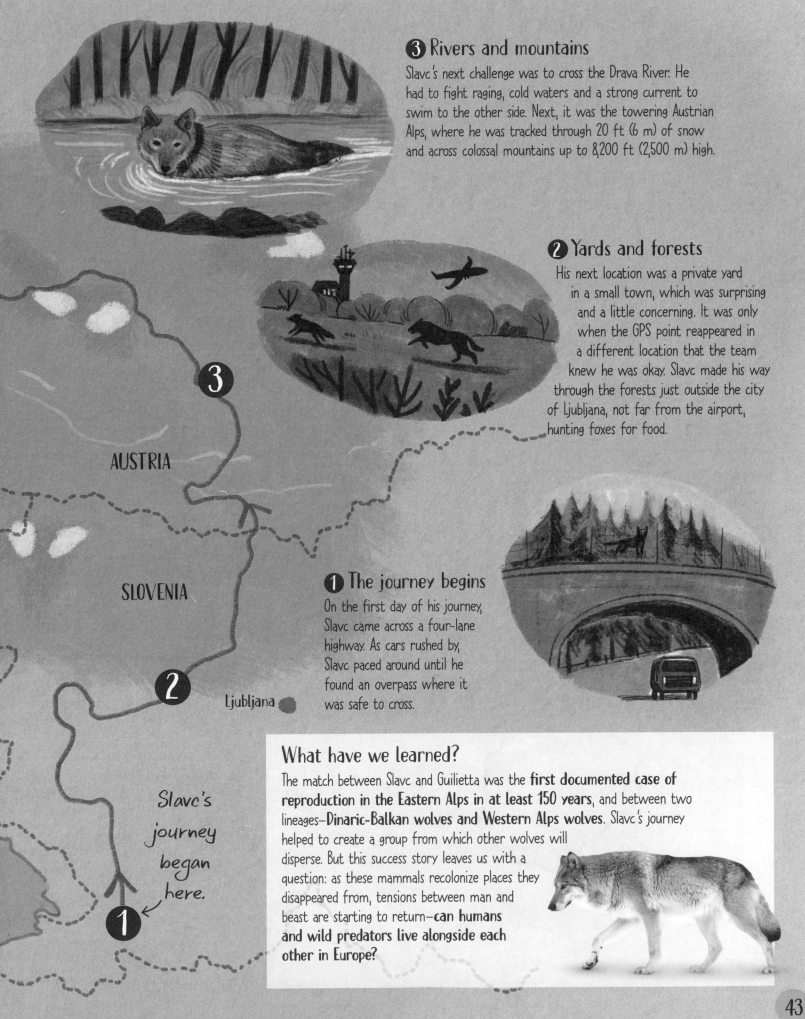

❸ Rivers and mountains

Slavc's next challenge was to cross the Drava River. He had to fight raging, cold waters and a strong current to swim to the other side. Next, it was the towering Austrian Alps, where he was tracked through 20 ft (6 m) of snow and across colossal mountains up to 8,200 ft (2,500 m) high.

❷ Yards and forests

His next location was a private yard in a small town, which was surprising and a little concerning. It was only when the GPS point reappeared in a different location that the team knew he was okay. Slavc made his way through the forests just outside the city of Ljubljana, not far from the airport, hunting foxes for food.

AUSTRIA

❸

SLOVENIA

❷

Ljubljana ●

❶ The journey begins

On the first day of his journey, Slavc came across a four-lane highway. As cars rushed by, Slavc paced around until he found an overpass where it was safe to cross.

Slavc's journey began here.

❶

What have we learned?

The match between Slavc and Guilietta was the **first documented case of reproduction in the Eastern Alps in at least 150 years**, and between two lineages–Dinaric-Balkan wolves and Western Alps wolves. Slavc's journey helped to create a group from which other wolves will disperse. But this success story leaves us with a question: as these mammals recolonize places they disappeared from, tensions between man and beast are starting to return–**can humans and wild predators live alongside each other in Europe?**

Gray wolves

The ancestors of domestic dogs, gray wolves are highly sociable animals that are found in North America, Asia, and Europe. Like all wolves, they are carnivores. They work together to hunt their prey and share it with the pack.

Wolf packs

Gray wolves live in packs as large as 24, but most often the packs number between six and 10. Wolves form strong social bonds and have a hierarchy within the pack to maintain order.

A pack contains an alpha male, an alpha female, and their young. The alphas are in charge, and each takes on a different role. The female will care for and defend her pups, and the male is in charge of finding and providing food.

Wolf packs have territories that can be as large as 1,150 sq miles (3,000 sq km). Wolves defend their territories fiercely.

With long legs, gray wolves can run up to 37 mph (60 kph).

Wolves have thick fur to keep them warm.

Slavc's collar
The collar used to track Slavc's movements had a GPS receiver that sent a signal every three hours, so scientists were able to keep track of his location in great detail.

Lone wolves

Although wolves are usually social, sometimes a wolf will leave its pack and **set out alone**, often looking for a place to begin a pack of its own. This process is known as dispersal. **Lone wolves must be careful not to trespass into other packs' territories and are known to search for hundreds of miles to find the best location.** Sometimes, a lone wolf succeeds in tracking down a mate and starting a new pack, but other times, they return to their original pack.

Large, pointed ears mean that wolves can hear prey from miles away.

Pack communication

Wolves communicate with each other visually, using **facial expressions, body positions, and tail positions, and through vocalizations and scent marking.** They also howl to stay in contact and strengthen their bonds as a pack and to let neighboring packs know not to intrude on their territory.

"It seemed like Puma 8 had reached a tiny island in the middle of a huge lake and returned to the mainland between his bouts of foraging."

Location: Patagonia
Species: Puma
Puma concolor

Puma 8
The swimming puma

Patagonia, in South America, is home to dramatic mountain landscapes that tower over southern beech forests, as streaks of orange and deep blue dance across the sky. Despite its beauty, Patagonia is a harsh place to live... unless you are a puma. The puma has been named "the King of the Ice Mountains", and one puma in particular stood out to a team of scientists working there: Puma 8. He showed another side to these iconic cats—a love of water!

Puma 8 and others

The puma is a cat with many names. They are called mountain lions, cougars, pumas, or panthers, depending on where they are found. In recent years, stories of swimming pumas have come to light, which might explain some of their hunting success as a big cat. Stories of others, alongside Puma 8, prove that these adventurous felines are confident in the water, even traveling long distances.

Pacific Ocean

What have we learned?
South America is a vast and complex landscape made up of raging rivers, ice fields, fjords, and giant lakes. Many would consider these environments as "barriers" for this species, but Puma 8 proves otherwise. The ability to overcome such barriers could actually explain the success of this species. Understanding how pumas interact with this wild landscape may help scientists better understand **how we can protect them across South America.**

❶ Patagonia
Scientists spent 10 months tracking Puma 8. Then one night, quite surprisingly, he set his sights on Isla Victor in the middle of Lago Cochrane. Visting the island to hunt, Puma 8 made five trips over one month. He never remained during daylight hours on any trip and consistently traveled to and from the island within a single night. The distances he swam ranged from 1,800 to 3,550ft (550 to 1080 m).

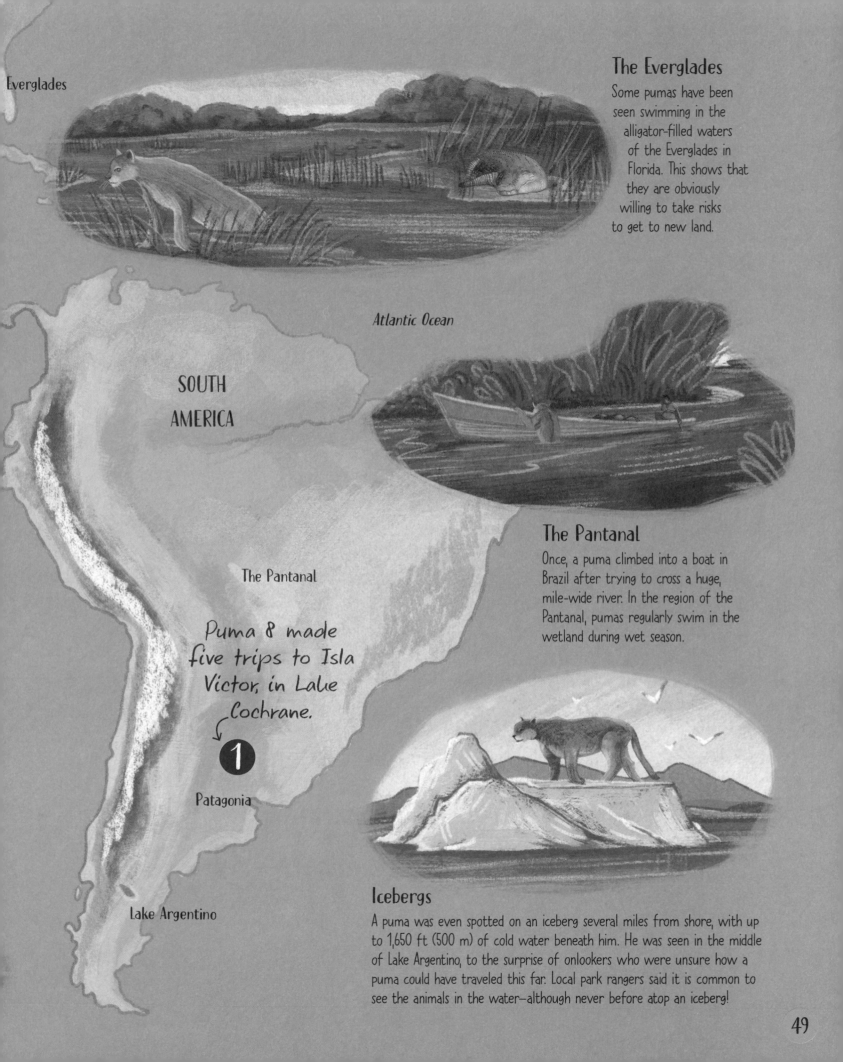

The Everglades
Some pumas have been seen swimming in the alligator-filled waters of the Everglades in Florida. This shows that they are obviously willing to take risks to get to new land.

Everglades

Atlantic Ocean

SOUTH AMERICA

The Pantanal

Puma 8 made five trips to Isla Victor, in Lake Cochrane.

1

Patagonia

Lake Argentino

The Pantanal
Once, a puma climbed into a boat in Brazil after trying to cross a huge, mile-wide river. In the region of the Pantanal, pumas regularly swim in the wetland during wet season.

Icebergs
A puma was even spotted on an iceberg several miles from shore, with up to 1,650 ft (500 m) of cold water beneath him. He was seen in the middle of Lake Argentino, to the surprise of onlookers who were unsure how a puma could have traveled this far. Local park rangers said it is common to see the animals in the water—although never before atop an iceberg!

Pumas

These large mountain cats roam from rocky landscapes to valleys and hillsides in search of territory. Mostly, they respect the territories of other cats. Despite being solitary animals, they are known to share their kills with others—it is unclear why, but research suggests this behavior is prompted by both social and biological factors.

The puma is one of the best jumpers in the cat family.

Mountain dweller

Pumas can be found across a huge range of North and South America, from Canada all the way down to Argentina. They prefer mountainous areas and hide behind rocks and boulders while hunting for prey. Pumas can be brown, pale gray, or a sandy color, all of which help them hide among the rocky terrain.

The long tail is usually held close to the ground when on the move.

The puma has the longest hind legs in relation to body size of all the big cats—it is also one of the best jumpers in the cat family.

The shade of the coat varies geographically as well as seasonally across all pumas.

A big house cat

Pumas are the **fourth largest cat in the world,** after the lion, tiger, and jaguar. Males can weigh up to 220 lb (100 kg), while females tend to weigh at least 100 lb (45 kg). They can measure 5-8¾ ft (1.5-2.7 m) in length. Pumas inhabiting lands near the equator are typically smaller than those farther to the north or south. Pumas do not roar like other big cats, but actually emit purring sounds, like a domestic cat.

Sharp, retractable claws also help the puma when climbing trees to escape from other predators.

Inspiring figure

Pumas are known to the Chilean locals as the **"Guardian of the Andes,"** and they can be found across the country, from the Atacama Desert to Patagonia. Although more densely populated in Chile, pumas are admired and respected by indigenous cultures all throughout the Americas. The people believe pumas are a sacred animal, much like condors and eagles.

Location: South Georgia

Species: Wandering albatross

Diomedea exulans

Sitka

The albatross supermom

This is the story of Sitka. Her name means "snow in the south" in Inuit. Born in 1986, Sitka is an impressive supermom, having successfully raised eight chicks. Tagged on the island of South Georgia and tracked by scientists, her story is full of twists and turns as she navigates being a modern-day albatross in a changing world.

"The wandering albatross is one of our planet's most impressive seabirds. A species that gracefully soars for days, even weeks, over thunderous Southern Ocean waves in search of food."

Sitka's flight track of one round trip: 6,520 miles (10,500 km).

SOUTH AMERICA

Atlantic Ocean

By dynamic soaring (riding on wind currents), albatrosses accomplish huge feats of long-distance flight.

South Georgia

This is where Sitka calls home.

Sitka's story

The island of South Georgia is home to a place called Bird Island Research Station. The scientists there tag and monitor the wandering albatrosses, as well as many of the penguin colonies found locally. A particularly special albatross studied here is an older female named Sitka.

Sitka and Ernest

Sitka met Ernest, a male albatross that hatched in 1997, and together they have successfully raised a number of chicks. Part of their role as a mating pair is making regular trips out to sea in search of food for their fast-growing chicks. On one known occasion, Sitka flew a round trip of about 6,520 miles (10,500 km) in just 16 days—that's longer than the Great Wall of China!

Sitka the Supermom

Wandering albatrosses breed every other year. Sitka was first tagged in 2020, when she had a chick named Nova. When Sitka came back, she and Ernest raised another chick named Endurance. Nova then fledged and was even seen taking off for the first time. In January 2023, Endurance also fledged successfully.

Out to sea

Every time Sitka goes out to sea to find food for her growing family, it provides the scientists with important data about her movements, particularly her interactions with fishing vessels. These vessels can be a danger to seabirds, so collecting this data is crucial work in the effort to conserve the birds' numbers.

Wandering albatrosses

Wandering albatrosses are one of the world's largest seabirds. They are pelagic, which means they spend most of their lives at sea, traveling enormous distances and only coming to land to feed and breed. Scientists first started to appreciate the astonishing distances these birds travel in the late 1980s, when they were able to track them by remote satellite.

The bill is light pink. →

Long-distance flight

Wandering albatrosses spend most of their lives in the air, and by riding on wind currents, they can cover huge distances without flapping their wings. They can even sleep while flying. It is thought that they fly the equivalent of 18 round trips to the moon and back in a lifetime.

Impressive birds

At a massive 11 ft (3.4 m), albatrosses have the largest wingspan of any bird. They can drink saltwater and live an average of 50 years in the wild. But perhaps their greatest feat is their ability to fly **thousands of miles for up to 45 days without landing.**

Wandering albatrosses
can fly up to 25 miles
(40 km) per hour.

The feathered breast and belly become pure white with age.

The black tips remain on the outer tail feathers.

Eating scraps

Wandering albatrosses are **opportunistic surface feeders.** They predominantly feed on fish and squid. The primary fish species in their diet is the Patagonian toothfish, sometimes eaten as discarded waste from fishing vessels.

Albatross conservation

Many of our seabirds, especially albatrosses, have experienced rapid population decline in recent decades. Unfortunately, they are one of the most threatened groups of birds on the planet, largely due to to the growing challenge of nets from fishing vessels.

Global cooperation

Sitka's journey has shown us that wandering albatrosses are a species that covers huge distances across vast expanses of ocean. **So, international cooperation is really important if we are to protect them.** We all need to work together to look after the wandering albatross, so that Sitka can return home safely every time she flies out to hunt for food. Fleets from all over the world go to the Southern Ocean to fish, and **this is where albatrosses encounter vessels and get into trouble.** Global Fishing Watch is working to make sure vessels are fishing legally.

Journal entry

Wind whips around the tussock grass. A bright rainbow shines over the inky Southern Ocean. Bird Island is a rugged rock on the north-west tip of the sub-Antarctic island of South Georgia. This island is also home to the wandering albatross. Rulers of these southern skies, the wandering albatross has the largest wingspan of any bird on the planet.

South Georgia is a convenient oasis near rich feeding grounds, where the Atlantic meets cold polar waters, isolated from land predators. In the height of summer, millions of penguins call this place home, along with snow petrels, prions, fulmars, and noisy fur seals. In summer, the beaches are jammed with life, while albatrosses dominate the skies.

Albatrosses are like downhill skiers, elegantly veering left and right with ease. Sitka delicately traces one wingtip along a wave and then banks abruptly, turning into a glide, with the wind howling at her tail. Our ship rolls in the wake of the wind. This creature could be older than me. I wonder what she's thinking about—her chick back on the island, her mate, the weather, or nothing at all?

Fishing vessels

Albatrosses are often attracted by the prospect of an easy meal of fish discards, and **careless fishing vessels play a part in the death of tens of thousands of albatrosses every year.** Bycatch is the word given to creatures accidentally trapped by fishing nets intended for a different species. Albatrosses become bycatch when they encounter baited hooks, get tangled in nets, or collide with warp cables when scavenging for food on the ocean's surface, and then ultimately drown. Luckily, there are efforts to **make fishing more sustainable** and reduce the risk of the unintentional death of these wonderful birds.

Location: Zambia and Mozambique

Species: African wild dog

Lycaon pictus

EWD 1355 and her sisters

The sisters on a mission

It was October 2021. Rain poured down on the Zambian landscape, and three brave African wild dogs peeled away from their pack and began a 1,300 mile (2,100 km) journey to forge a new dynasty. Over nine months, they crossed raging rivers, escaped poachers and predators, and ventured into new territories. The sisters set a new record for distance traveled in the pursuit of a new home.

"Somehow, against all odds, these sisters not only survived, but thrived as a pack of three. "

EWD 1355's journey

As rains fell and the banks of rivers burst all across Zambia, EWD 1355, a female African wild dog, and her two sisters left their pack in the Luangwa Valley in the east of the country. Their mission was to start a new pack, and they were about to embark on an unforgettable journey.

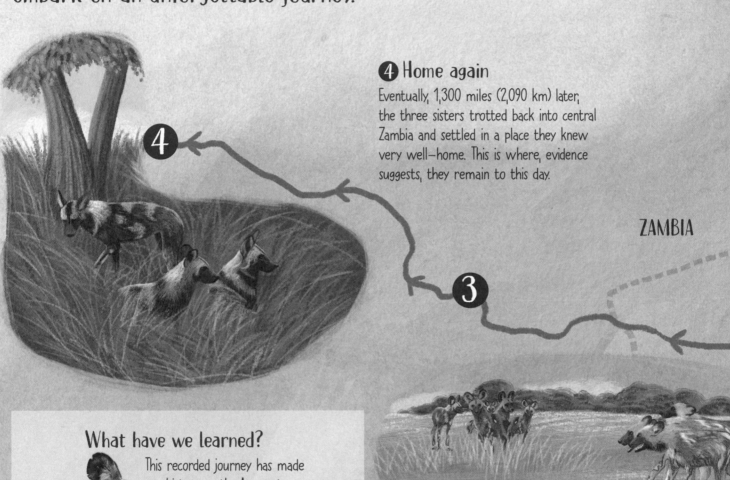

4 Home again
Eventually, 1,300 miles (2,090 km) later, the three sisters trotted back into central Zambia and settled in a place they knew very well—home. This is where, evidence suggests, they remain to this day.

ZAMBIA

What have we learned?
This recorded journey has made history as the **longest-ever distance continuously traveled by any pack of African wild dogs**. Along the way, the three sisters faced a range of natural, ecological, and human threats such as **armed hunters, poacher traps, and busy communities**. This journey provides us with an understanding of how it might be possible to better protect this endangered species.

3 The encounter
The sisters headed back to their birth country, and toward the Lower Zambezi National Park. This is the home of the Zambezi wild dogs, who have mastered hunting African buffalo—prey that few wild dogs dare approach. Over the next few months, they followed the Zambezi pack, but never managed to oust the alpha female, and were outnumbered. So, it was time to move on.

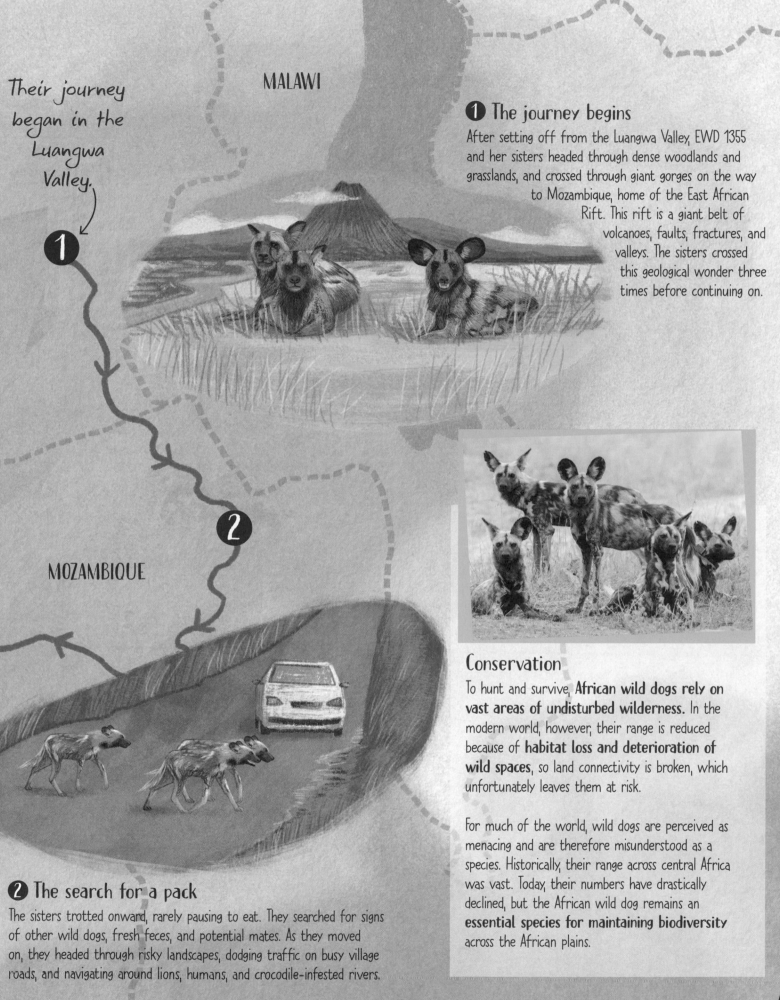

Their journey began in the Luangwa Valley.

1

MALAWI

1 The journey begins

After setting off from the Luangwa Valley, EWD 1355 and her sisters headed through dense woodlands and grasslands, and crossed through giant gorges on the way to Mozambique, home of the East African Rift. This rift is a giant belt of volcanoes, faults, fractures, and valleys. The sisters crossed this geological wonder three times before continuing on.

2

MOZAMBIQUE

Conservation

To hunt and survive, **African wild dogs rely on vast areas of undisturbed wilderness.** In the modern world, however, their range is reduced because of **habitat loss and deterioration of wild spaces**, so land connectivity is broken, which unfortunately leaves them at risk.

For much of the world, wild dogs are perceived as menacing and are therefore misunderstood as a species. Historically, their range across central Africa was vast. Today, their numbers have drastically declined, but the African wild dog remains an **essential species for maintaining biodiversity** across the African plains.

2 The search for a pack

The sisters trotted onward, rarely pausing to eat. They searched for signs of other wild dogs, fresh feces, and potential mates. As they moved on, they headed through risky landscapes, dodging traffic on busy village roads, and navigating around lions, humans, and crocodile-infested rivers.

African wild dogs

African wild dogs are striking. Rich amber eyes, white-tipped tails, and disk-shaped ears all make this species both colorful and unique. Their historical range is huge, cutting across central Africa. Unfortunately, the drastic decline in their numbers has made the African wild dog one of the world's most endangered mammals.

Chatty

African wild dogs are a very vocal species. When they chat to one another they **twitter, chirp, and hoot like birds**. Despite all this communication, they do not utilize the body language or facial expressions that are seen in other members of the dog family.

Deadly hunters

African wild dogs are some of Africa's most successful hunters. When traveling, they move with speed, trotting single file at dawn and dusk to avoid the heat of the day. They usually target weaker individuals in a herd. Wild dogs have stamina on their side, often running their prey to exhaustion. This simple but efficient strategy means 80 percent of their hunts end in a successful kill—a higher success rate than even lions!

Their thick fur keeps them warm at night.

African wild dogs do not have dewclaws (similar to thumbs or big toes) and tend to have fused middle-toe pads.

Not only do the characteristically large ears swivel like satellite dishes to listen for prey, but they also help to keep the dogs cool in the hot habitat of the African plains.

Family units

African wild dogs are efficient and powerful, often working as a hunting pack sometimes 20-strong. They have a **tight-knit social structure** that shows a softer side to this species. They have strong social bonds and look out for one another, whether that be old, young, or injured pack members.

"Everything about John Coe is fascinating. He has a sloped eye patch and is a large ecotype of orca. But most impressive of all is his towering notched dorsal fin that cuts through the inky Scottish seas."

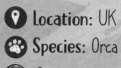 Location: UK

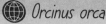 Species: Orca

🌐 *Orcinus orca*

John Coe and Aquarius

The last of their pod

John Coe, an impressive male orca, is one of the last of his kind. He belongs to the West Coast Community pod, and can be found roaming UK waters. This is the story of how he and Aquarius, the last two surviving members of their pod, connected with coastal communities across Britain through a surprising and extraordinary journey.

John Coe's movements

In the spring of 2021, much of the UK was captivated by a sighting of John Coe and Aquarius off the western tip of Cornwall. Communities along the UK coastline were hooked, keeping an eye on the horizon for the two iconic dorsal fins cutting through the water. Little did they know that this was the wrong place to look—just nine days later, the orcas were spotted off the Isle of Skye in Scotland, after traveling 550 miles (885 km) in just over one week. What an extraordinary journey!

❶ Surprise guests

The wild seas that meet the rugged coasts of Cornwall boast impressive marine life. Blue fin tuna and migratory species such as blue sharks are regular residents, but locals were shocked when John Coe and Aquarius paid a visit. Easily identifiable John Coe has a distinct notch in his dorsal fin and an injury on his tail fluke, most likely from a shark attack.

Atlantic Ocean

NORTHE
IRELAN

IRELAND

The West Coast Community pod

Orcas are split up into ecotypes depending on their habitat, behavior, and diet. John Coe and Aquarius are an ecotype known as North Atlantic Type 2, which is specific to their pod. Since 1994, the West Coast Community pod has been documented around the British Isles. **They are a resident orca pod that tends to feed on fish.** These are typically less aggressive than transient orca pods, which hunt in teams for larger prey such as seals. Over time, the number of individuals sighted from the pod has plummeted, and just two males now remain. **Sadly, without any females to mate with, this ecotype of orca will become extinct after John Coe and Aquarius pass away.**

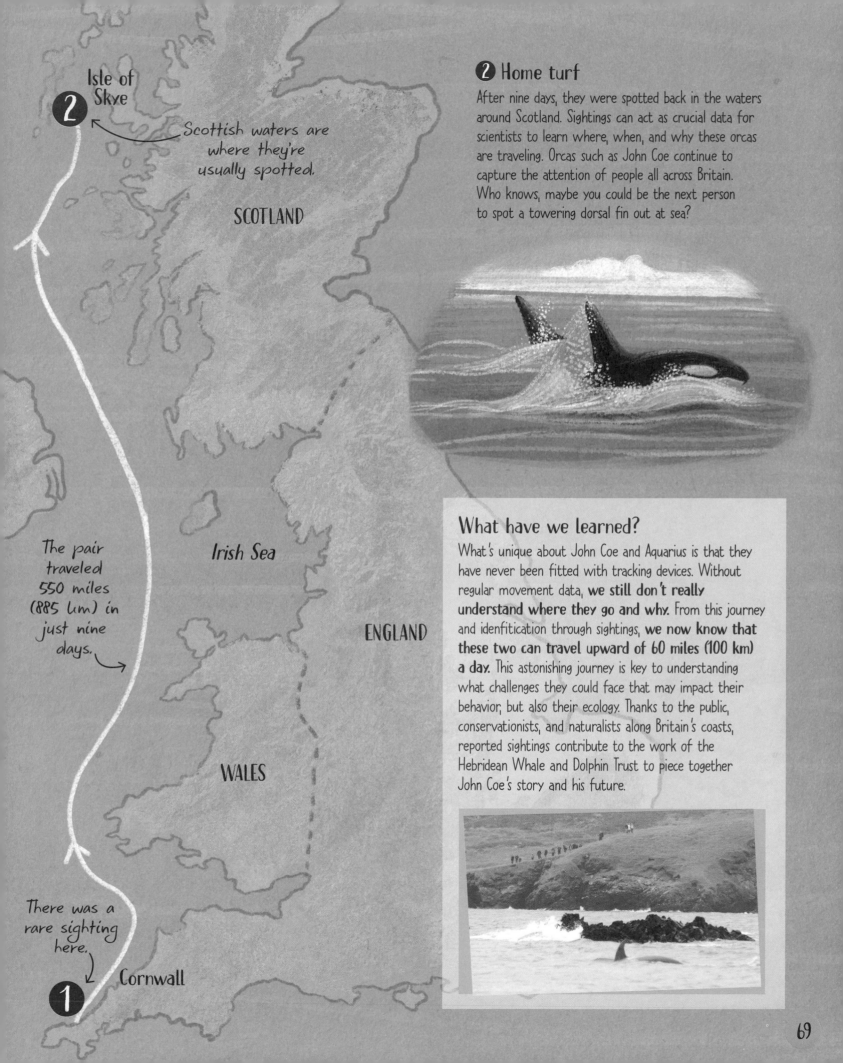

Isle of Skye

② Isle of Skye

Scottish waters are where they're usually spotted.

SCOTLAND

② Home turf

After nine days, they were spotted back in the waters around Scotland. Sightings can act as crucial data for scientists to learn where, when, and why these orcas are traveling. Orcas such as John Coe continue to capture the attention of people all across Britain. Who knows, maybe you could be the next person to spot a towering dorsal fin out at sea?

The pair traveled 550 miles (885 km) in just nine days.

Irish Sea

ENGLAND

What have we learned?

What's unique about John Coe and Aquarius is that they have never been fitted with tracking devices. Without regular movement data, **we still don't really understand where they go and why.** From this journey and idenfitication through sightings, **we now know that these two can travel upward of 60 miles (100 km) a day.** This astonishing journey is key to understanding what challenges they could face that may impact their behavior, but also their ecology. Thanks to the public, conservationists, and naturalists along Britain's coasts, reported sightings contribute to the work of the Hebridean Whale and Dolphin Trust to piece together John Coe's story and his future.

WALES

There was a rare sighting here.

① Cornwall

Orcas

Orcas, despite being called killer whales, are actually the biggest members of the dolphin family. They can be found in all of the world's oceans living in close-knit family groups called pods, which are usually led by a female.

Orcas hold their breath underwater for up to 15 minutes, and only begin to exhale through the blowhole just before they come up to the surface.

Grandmothers

Female orcas are known to live for as long as 90 years, almost double the 50-year life expectancy of males. Because they stop reproducing at around age 40, this means that **some females live to see grandcalves born into their family.** Studies have shown that calves with grandmothers survive longer than those without. Orca pods are matriarchal (led by females), so scientists believe that these older females share crucial survival skills with their younger relatives, perhaps making a difference between life and death.

Echolocation

Orcas are intelligent and social animals, using echolocation to communicate with each other and coordinate their pods while hunting. They make a series of sounds underwater (such as clicks and whistles) that travel toward their prey. When the sound waves hit the animal, they bounce back to the orca to reveal its size, location, and movements. **Orcas across the world have different hunting tactics, and even different dialects from pod to pod.**

Females have a smaller dorsal fin than males. →

Pack hunter

Orcas can hunt in large and efficient groups of up to 40 family members, much like a wolf pack. They carry out coordinated attacks that are extremely effective in taking down their prey. They use different tactics to hunt for the wide variety of animals that make up their diet. Being at the top of the food chain, they are spoiled for choice. Fish, penguins, and marine mammals such as seals are all on the menu.

A streamlined body shape is energy-efficient, creating less resistance in the water.

The strong jaw and teeth are adapted to tear, rather than chew, prey.

Orca conservation

Orcas face numerous threats. These include everything from the influence of climate change to more direct impacts such as fishing entanglement, plastic and noise pollution, and sharing waters with an increasing amount of human activity. Orcas are one of the most widespread cetaceans on the planet, found in warm tropical waters and polar regions, so it's important that we protect them.

Clean up our oceans

In 2016, Lulu, the last female from the UK's West Coast Community pod, was found washed up on the Isle of Tiree, Scotland. **Unfortunately, she had died after getting entangled in fishing gear.** After examination, scientists found that **her body was highly contaminated with PCBs – chemicals that come from plastic pollution.** She was noted to be at least 20 years old, but she had never had any calves. Scientists believe this was why. It's not too late for you to become a citizen scientist and join the movement to help this pod and others, starting by joining local efforts to **clean up our oceans and rid them of plastic.**

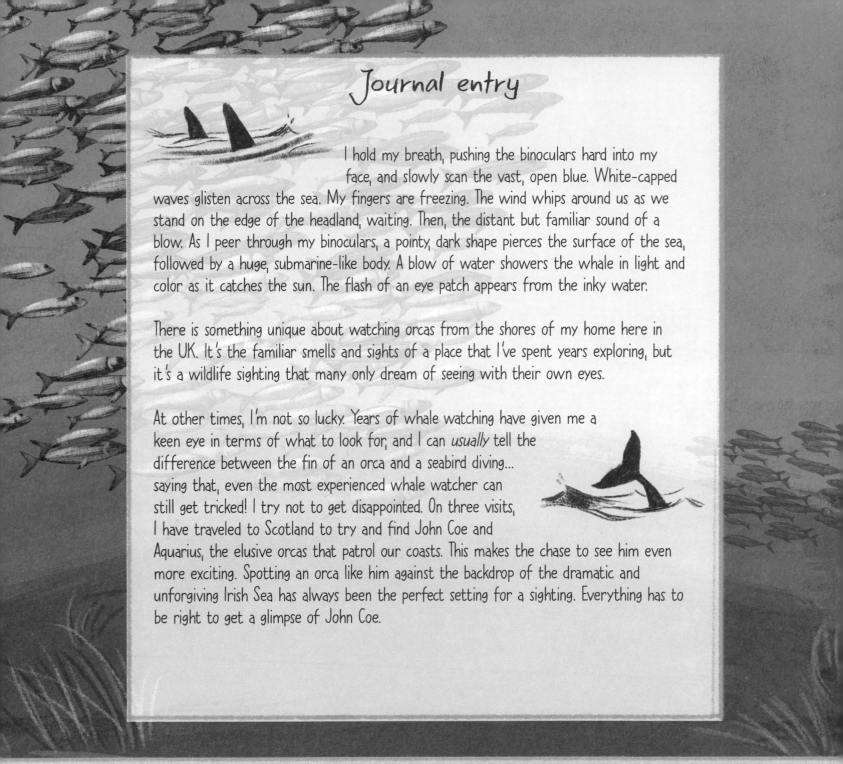

Journal entry

I hold my breath, pushing the binoculars hard into my face, and slowly scan the vast, open blue. White-capped waves glisten across the sea. My fingers are freezing. The wind whips around us as we stand on the edge of the headland, waiting. Then, the distant but familiar sound of a blow. As I peer through my binoculars, a pointy, dark shape pierces the surface of the sea, followed by a huge, submarine-like body. A blow of water showers the whale in light and color as it catches the sun. The flash of an eye patch appears from the inky water.

There is something unique about watching orcas from the shores of my home here in the UK. It's the familiar smells and sights of a place that I've spent years exploring, but it's a wildlife sighting that many only dream of seeing with their own eyes.

At other times, I'm not so lucky. Years of whale watching have given me a keen eye in terms of what to look for, and I can *usually* tell the difference between the fin of an orca and a seabird diving... saying that, even the most experienced whale watcher can still get tricked! I try not to get disappointed. On three visits, I have traveled to Scotland to try and find John Coe and Aquarius, the elusive orcas that patrol our coasts. This makes the chase to see him even more exciting. Spotting an orca like him against the backdrop of the dramatic and unforgiving Irish Sea has always been the perfect setting for a sighting. Everything has to be right to get a glimpse of John Coe.

Global efforts

I have witnessed orcas hunting everything from humpback whales in the icy Southern Ocean, to a 20-strong pod breaking up a ball of herring fish in the Arctic. Luckily, we recognize how important orcas are, so they are a **highly protected species** across much of the world. **Orcas are a crucial indicator species**—they serve as a good measure of the health of an environment. They play an important role in **maintaining the ocean food chain, recycling nutrients, and regulating our climate**. If we want to have continued healthy marine ecosystems, we need to do all that we can to protect this species.

Glossary

Apex predator
Animal at the top of its food chain that has no natural predators

Archipelago
Group of islands

Cetacean
Marine mammal such as a whale, dolphin, or porpoise

Deforestation
Destruction of forests

Denning
Building and staying in a den or place of shelter

Dewclaw
Digit on the forelimbs of some animals, like a thumb

Disperse
Moving away from the area in which an animal was born and settling, and often reproducing, somewhere new

Distinctive
Characteristic that serves to distinguish an animal or person from others

Distribution
Something being spread over an area or shared among a group

Dynasty
Powerful group of animals that is often related and in charge of a larger group

Ecological
Concerned with the interactions between species in their natural environment

Ecosystem
Community of living things and their environment

Ecotype
Group of animals or plants that are found in a specific habitat but look or act differently from other members of their species found elsewhere

Elusive
Difficult to see, catch, or find in the wild

Encroach
To intrude on territory

Fjord
Strip of sea that comes into the land between high cliffs and that was created by glaciers

Flank
Side of the body, between the ribs and the hip

Flehmening
Curling of the upper lip and raising of the head in some mammals in response to smells

Foraging
Searching widely for provisions, namely food

Forepaws
Front paws of a four-footed animal

Geological
Relating to Earth science and how the Earth was formed, including its structure and composition

GPS
Global Positioning System. This satellite-based radio navigation system is used to track location

Hammock forest
Small "island" of forested high ground in a wetland habitat

Hierarchy
Order of who is in charge, for example, animals being ruled by alpha members of the group

Ice floe
Large piece of ice floating in the sea

Indicator species
Species that reflects the specific environment in which it lives; used to monitor ecosystems

Indigenous
Native to a particular place

Keystone species
Animal or plant species that is crucial to holding an ecosystem together

Prehistoric
Existing at a time before information was written down

Resident pod
Orca pod that is usually large in number and contains extended family members; the pod preys mainly on fish

Recolonize
Become reestablished in an area from which a species had previously disappeared

Retractable
Drawn back when not in use

Scent marking
Distinctive odor, from urine or another liquid, deposited by an animal; it functions as an identifying signal to other animals of the species

Site fidelity
Animal's ability to return to a previously visited location

Stronghold
Location that holds a larger number of a species than anywhere else

Transient pod
Orca pod that is small in number than usual and that uses aggressive pack-hunting techniques to prey on mammals as well as fish

Transmitter
Item used to send signals or process information. These signals can contain audio, video, or data

Vocalization
Noise made by the mouth or nose of an animal to communicate

Index

Acknowledgements

DK would like to thank Sif Nørskov and Syed Md Farhan for additional design, Simon Mumford for cartography assistance, and Phil Hunt for proofing.

The publisher would like to thank the following for their kind permission to reproduce their photographs:

(Key: a-above; b-below/bottom; c-center; f-far; l-left; r-right; t-top)

5 Dreamstime.com: Sergii Moskaliuk / Seregam (Paper). Getty Images: Johnny Johnson. 10 Getty Images: Paul Souders (br). 11 Alamy Stock Photo: Flip Nicklin / Minden Pictures (br). Dreamstime.com: Sergii Moskaliuk / Seregam (t). 12 Dreamstime.com: Sergii Moskaliuk / Seregam; Ana Vasileva (cb). 15 Dreamstime.com: Uwe Bergwitz (tc); Sergii Moskaliuk / Seregam. naturepl.com: Nick Gordon (cb). 16 Alamy Stock Photo: Waterframe_fba (cl). Dreamstime.com: Sergii Moskaliuk / Seregam (bl, tr). 16-17 Alamy Stock Photo: imageBROKER.com GmbH & Co. KG / Erich Schmidt. 17 Dreamstime.com: Sergii Moskaliuk / Seregam (cr). 18 www.mediadrumworld.com: Dreamstime.com: Sergii Moskaliuk / Seregam (t). 20 Dreamstime.com: Sergii Moskaliuk / Seregam. Shutterstock.com: Tomas Kotouc (cb). 22 Dreamstime.com: Sergii Moskaliuk / Seregam (bl). Getty Images: by wildestanimal (cl). 24-25 Alamy Stock Photo: Wildestanimal. Dreamstime.com: Sergii Moskaliuk / Seregam (Paper). 25 Alamy Stock Photo: Media Drum World (br). 26 Alamy Stock Photo: ArteSub (bl). 27 Dreamstime.com: Sergii Moskaliuk / Seregam (t). naturepl.com: Doug Perrine (bl). 28 Alamy Stock Photo: Matthias Breiter / Minden Pictures (cb). Dreamstime.com: Sergii Moskaliuk / Seregam. 31 Dreamstime.com: Sergii Moskaliuk / Seregam (tr, b). naturepl.com: Hiroya Minakuchi (bl). 32-33 Dreamstime.com: Tloventures. 33 Dreamstime.com: Sergii Moskaliuk / Seregam. 35 Alamy Stock Photo: Genevieve Vallee (cb). Dreamstime.com: Sergii Moskaliuk / Seregam. 37 Dreamstime.com: Sergii Moskaliuk / Seregam (b). Getty Images: Mike Korostelev (bl). 38-39 Alamy Stock Photo: SeaTops. 39 Dreamstime.com: Sergii Moskaliuk / Seregam. 41 Dreamstime.com: Vasyl Helevachuk (cb); Sergii Moskaliuk / Seregam. 43 Dreamstime.com: Maria Itina (br/Wolf); Sergii Moskaliuk / Seregam (br). 44-45 Dreamstime.com: Sergii Moskaliuk / Seregam. Getty Images: Raimund Linke (b). 44 Alamy Stock Photo: Yva Momatiuk & John Eastcott / Minden Pictures (bl). 47 Dreamstime.com: Maria Itina (cb); Sergii Moskaliuk / Seregam. 48 Dreamstime.com: Sergii Moskaliuk / Seregam (bl). naturepl.com: Ingo Arndt (cl). 50-51 Alamy Stock Photo: Senior Mac Photography. Shutterstock.com: Jan Jerman (b). 51 Dreamstime.com: Sergii Moskaliuk / Seregam. 52 Alamy Stock Photo: Max Allen (cb). Dreamstime.com: Sergii Moskaliuk / Seregam. 56 Alamy Stock Photo: David Tipling Photo Library (cl/Bird). Dreamstime.com: Sergii Moskaliuk / Seregam (cl). 56-57 Alamy Stock Photo: Helmut Corneli (b); Philip Mugridge. 57 Dreamstime.com: Sergii Moskaliuk / Seregam (cr). 58 Alamy Stock Photo: Barry Bland (br). 59 Dreamstime.com: Sergii Moskaliuk / Seregam (t). Getty Images: wildestanimal (br). 60 Alamy Stock Photo: Ariadne Van Zandbergen (cb). Dreamstime.com: Sergii Moskaliuk / Seregam. 62 Alamy Stock Photo: Christopher Scott (bl/dog). Dreamstime.com: Sergii Moskaliuk / Seregam (bl). 63 Alamy Stock Photo: Saverio Gatto (cl). Dreamstime.com: Sergii Moskaliuk / Seregam (br). 64 Alamy Stock Photo: Arco / TUNS / Imagebroker (cb). Dreamstime.com: Sergii Moskaliuk / Seregam (cl). Shutterstock.com: Thomas Retterath (crb). 65 Alamy Stock Photo: Denis-Huot / Nature Picture Library (l). Dreamstime.com: Sergii Moskaliuk / Seregam (cr). 67 Dreamstime.com: Sergii Moskaliuk / Seregam. Getty Images / iStock: longtaildog (cb). 68 Dreamstime.com: Sergii Moskaliuk / Seregam (b). naturepl.com: Chris Gomersall (br). 69 Alamy Stock Photo: Jack Perks (br). Dreamstime.com: Sergii Moskaliuk / Seregam (cr). 70 Dreamstime.com: Sergii Moskaliuk / Seregam (cl). 70-71 Shutterstock.com: Tory Kallman. 71 Dreamstime.com: Sergii Moskaliuk / Seregam (t). 72 Alamy Stock Photo: WaterFrame_fba (br). 73 Alamy Stock Photo: Hiroya Minakuchi / Minden Pictures (br). Dreamstime.com: Sergii Moskaliuk / Seregam (t). 74-75 Alamy Stock Photo: Helmut Corneli (b). 77 Dreamstime.com: Sergii Moskaliuk / Seregam (b). 78-79 Dreamstime.com: Sergii Moskaliuk / Seregam

Cover images: Back: Alamy Stock Photo: imageBROKER.com GmbH & Co. KG / Erich Schmidt cl; Spine: Dreamstime.com: Ana Vasileva t

All other images © Dorling Kindersley Limited

About this book

My job as a conservation filmmaker and scientist is to tell stories about the natural world—to uncover the hidden secrets of our planet, and document how our rapidly changing world is impacting its wildlife. Despite huge advances in technology and pioneering research, there is still so much we don't know about what species get up to in the wild. However, sometimes—just sometimes—we get a small, wonderful glimpse into what their lives are like, that helps us tell the tales of our planet's most curious wildlife species.

Throughout the pages of this book, we have followed in the footprints of polar bears, pumas, and jaguars, and explored the oceans with whales, seals, and seabirds. These are tales of migration, mystery, and unique behaviors—some that still puzzle scientists today. These tagged, tracked, and documented species showcase the stories of exceptional individual animals, who have taught us new and exciting information about their behavior and ecology, and helped scientists like me understand how to better conserve them and their habitats.

This book is a cross between science, storytelling, adventure, and conservation. It highlights the struggles that animals endure to feed, migrate, and survive. It also reminds us of the fragility of our natural world, and how important it is to care for our planet and to conserve these species. Showcasing stories of both iconic and more endangered species, the focus of this book is to bring you, the reader, on a journey through the eyes of a scientist.

Some stories include tales of well-documented individuals that have captured the hearts and minds of the general public, while others show their journey step-by-step. I ask you not to just view these dots and lines as maps, but as stories of the individual animals, with tales that inspire curiosity about their lives in the wild.

Lizzie Daly

About the author

Lizzie Daly is a scientist, wildlife TV host, and filmmaker. She was born in Germany but grew up in Wales. In the UK, she is regularly seen on the BBC as a wildlife host, but is also a face of the broadcast channel *Love Nature*. Her series *Deep Dive Australia* aired globally in 2023, including on Sky Nature in the UK. In 2024, Lizzie is filming two new series, one for the BBC, and another across North America for *Love Nature's* second series.

The author would like to thank

This book wouldn't exist without a number of incredibly thoughtful and supportive people in my life, including:

My closest family, my Mom, Dad, Jess, Meg, and my extended family. I am forever indebted to you for listening to my endless ideas, struggles, and successes in this process.

To my life-long friends Bec, Arun, Laura, Rowan, and Liv, who have always been so supportive of my career and know exactly how to make me feel at home, even in all the chaos.

To my friends Nicki, Erin, Dan, Bertie, Steve, Sarah, Ben, Mary. A few too many names to mention, but thank you for continuing to push me to grow and be better—always. Thank you.

To my agent Jo Sarsby, who I am always in awe of, and the incredible team in the office, including Haley and Robyn. You have always gone above and beyond to support me in my career, and pushed me in ways I can only dream of.

To my editor James Mitchem, and the DK team, who every step of the way have made this idea come to life—offering insight, encouragement, and patience at all the right times, from conception to publication. Also to the illustrator, Chiara, who made me fall in love with each character in the book, and who inspired me through my writing.

To my supervisors Rory and Luca, who have had a massive influence on my career path and have only ever been hugely supportive of me, even when trying to spin all the plates and needing additional time.

To all the women in science who came before me and paved the way for aspiring women in science like myself. To naturalists such as Joyce Poole, Jane Goodall, Sylvia Earle, and Christina Mittermeier, who I continue to look up to. Your dedication is what drives me to this day.

Further acknowledgements and study references

Polar Bear 20741
U.S. Geological Survey and University of Wyoming researchers, including USGS research zoologist George Durner, Professor Andrew Derocher, pilot Mike Woodcock, and the study's lead author, Nick Pilfold.

Mango
The Oncafari conservation team.

Harry Lindo
Nova Southeastern University's Guy Harvey Research Institute in Florida, in collaboration with the Bermuda Shark Project.

Bigonia
The Costa Lab, studying the ecology, physiology, and conservation of marine animals.

Tiny Tim
The crocodile tracking program conducted by the Franklin Eco-laboratory at the University of Queensland.

Slavc
Hubert Potočnik, the biologist whose work made this possible, and his colleagues at the University of Ljubljana in Slovenia.

Puma 8
The puma monitoring program, with the support of NatGeo and the University of California-Davis.

Sitka
Global Fishing Watch, BAS, DEFRA, and the Bird Island Team.

EWD 1355
The Zambian Carnivore Program.

John Coe & Aquarius
The Hebridean Whale and Dolphin Trust.

Author Lizzie Daly
Illustrator Chiara Fedele
Consultant Dr. Nick Crumpton

Senior Acquisitions Editor James Mitchem
Editors Abi Maxwell, Becca Arlington
US Editor Margaret Parrish
US Senior Editor Shannon Beatty
Senior Designer Claire Patane
Designer Tory Gordon-Harris
Managing Art Editor and Jacket Designer Elle Ward
Production Editor Becky Fallowfield
Production Controller Rebecca Parton
Senior Picture Researcher Sakshi Saluja
Jacket Coordinator Elin Woosnam
Art Director Mabel Chan

First American Edition, 2024
Published in the United States by DK Publishing,
a division of Penguin Random House LLC
1745 Broadway, 20th Floor, New York, NY 10019

DK books are available at special discounts when purchased
in bulk for sales promotions, premiums, fund-raising,
or educational use.
For details, contact: DK Publishing Special Markets,
1745 Broadway, 20th Floor, New York, NY 10019
SpecialSales@dk.com

Printed and bound in China

www.dk.com

This book was made with Forest
Stewardship Council™ certified
paper – one small step in DK's
commitment to a sustainable future.
Learn more at **www.dk.com/uk/**
information/sustainability